Science in Infographics
LIGHT AND SOUND

Jon Richards
and Ed Simkins

Gareth Stevens

Please visit our website, www.garethstevens.com.
For a free color catalog of all our high-quality books,
call toll free 1-800-542-2595 or fax 1-877-542-2596.

Cataloging-in-Publication Data

Names: Richards, Jon. | Simkins, Ed.
Title: Light and sound / Jon Richards and Ed Simkins.
Description: New York : Gareth Stevens Publishing, 2020. | Series: Science in
infographics | Includes glossary and index.
Identifiers: ISBN 9781538242919 (pbk.) | ISBN 9781538242933 (library bound) |
ISBN 9781538242926 (6 pack)
Subjects: LCSH: Light--Juvenile literature. | Sound--Juvenile literature. |
Information visualization--Juvenile literature.
Classification: LCC QC360.R47 2020 | DDC 535--dc23

Published in 2020 by
Gareth Stevens Publishing
111 East 14th Street, Suite 349
New York, NY 10003

Printed in the United States of America

CPSIA compliance information: Batch #CS19GS: For further information contact Gareth Stevens,
New York, New York at 1-800-542-2595.

CONTENTS

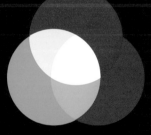

SOUND WAVES

Sounds are all around us, from the quiet rustle of leaves in the wind, to the roar of a jet plane taking off, or the beautiful music played by an instrument. All of these sounds are created by objects vibrating very quickly.

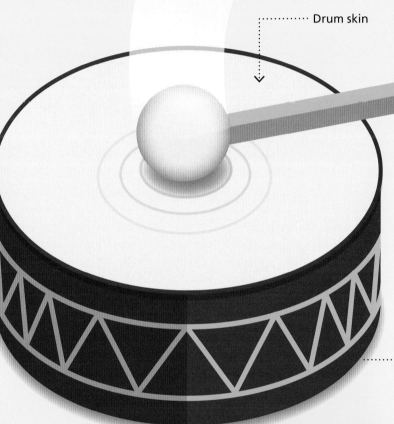

Drum skin

TRAVELING SOUNDS

When objects vibrate, they cause tiny molecules in the air to vibrate and knock into each other. This passes on the vibrations to the next molecule and the sounds spread out like ripples on a pond, until they reach your ears (see pages 28–29).

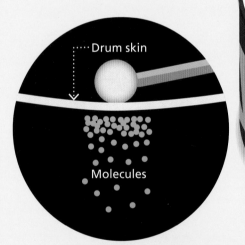

Drum skin

Molecules

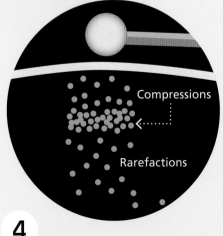

Compressions

Rarefactions

As the molecules vibrate, they create areas where they are squeezed together, called compressions, and areas where they are stretched out, called rarefactions.

Sound cannot travel through space because there are no molecules to vibrate.

A SOUND WAVE HAS DIFFERENT CHARACTERISTICS:

AMPLITUDE
This is the height of the sound wave. Loud sounds have a large amplitude with tall peaks, while quiet sounds have a small amplitude and short peaks.

WAVELENGTH
This is the distance between two peaks in the waves.

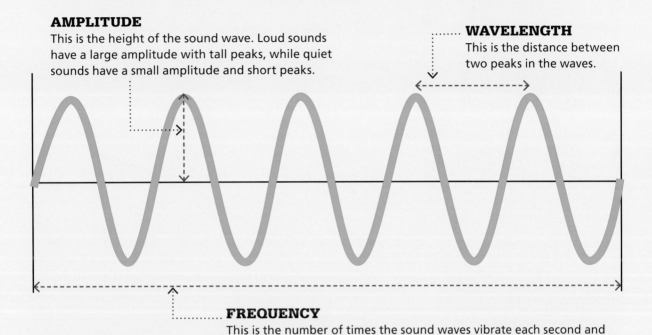

FREQUENCY
This is the number of times the sound waves vibrate each second and it determines how high or low a sound is. High-pitched sounds have a high frequency, while low-pitched sounds have a low frequency.

Compressions

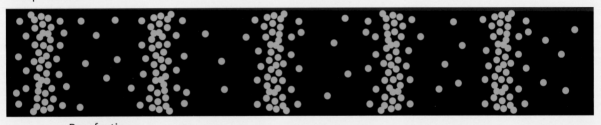

Rarefactions

Sound Types
The sort of sound you hear is determined by its tone, or timbre. This is the nature of the sound and helps you to tell a violin from a flute. Each instrument will create its own sound wave shape.

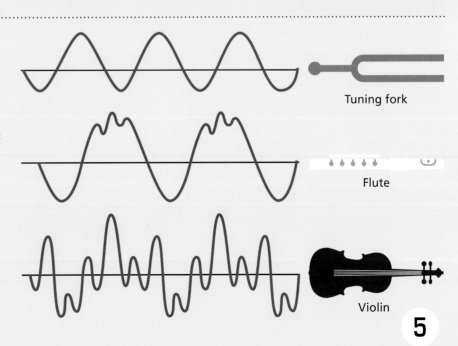

Tuning fork

Flute

Violin

LOUD AND QUIET

The loudness of a sound is called the volume. This is determined by the amplitude of the sound wave.

MEASURING VOLUME

The intensity of a sound is usually measured in units called decibels (dB). It is a logarithmic scale, which means it goes up in bigger and bigger steps. Near silence is 0 dB. A sound that is 10 times more powerful is 10 dB, a sound that is 100 times more powerful is 20 dB, and a sound that is 1,000 times more powerful is 30 dB.

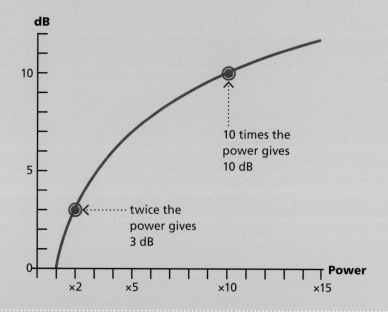

10 times the power gives 10 dB

twice the power gives 3 dB

Power

×2 ×5 ×10 ×15

Humans can hear sounds that range from almost near silence to a jet engine, which is about

1,000,000,000,000

times more powerful than near silence!

0dB silence (threshold of hearing)

20dB a quiet recording studio

60dB normal conversation

HERE ARE SOME OF THE LOUDEST ANIMALS ON THE PLANET

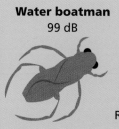

Water boatman
99 dB

Elephant
Rumbles recorded at 103 dB

Greengrocer cicada
120 dB

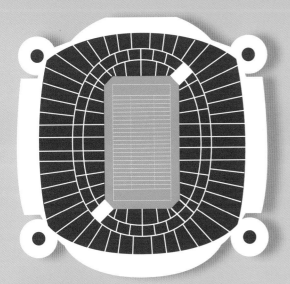

When the volcano of **Krakatoa** in Indonesia erupted in **1883,** the explosion was so loud that it was heard about **3,000 miles** (4,800 km) away on the island of Rodrigues near Mauritius in the Indian Ocean.

Superloud
The loudest crowd roar at a sports stadium was made at Arrowhead Stadium in Kansas City, Missouri, on September 29, 2014, when fans shouted at **142.2 dB**.

70dB loud phone ring

100dB electric saw

120dB close to a jet engine

Greater bulldog bat
Cries at 140 dB

Snapping shrimp
Screams measuring 200 dB

Blue whale
Clicks are measured at 230 dB

HIGH AND LOW

The pitch of a note is how high or low it sounds. It is decided by the number of times the sound source vibrates, which is known as the frequency.

Vibrating strings

Stringed instruments, such as a guitar, use strings of different thickness and tightness. Players then use their fingers to change the length of the part of the string that vibrates. This changes the pitch of the note.

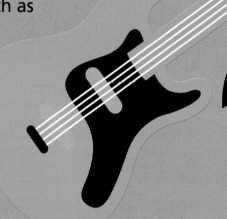

Plucked string vibrates

A plucked or bowed string vibrates at a certain frequency to play a certain note.

The pitch or frequency of a note is measured in hertz (Hz), which is the number of times it vibrates each second.

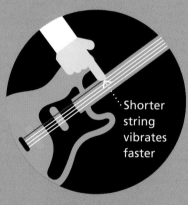

Shorter string vibrates faster

Shortening the string will produce a higher note. Halving the length means the string will vibrate twice as fast and play a note an octave higher.

Octave

| 27.5 Hz | 55 Hz | 110 Hz | 220 Hz | 440 Hz | 880 Hz | 1,760 Hz | 3,520 Hz |

PIANO KEYBOARD SHOWING FREQUENCIES OF THE NOTE "A"

Wind instruments alter the length and size of a vibrating column of air to play higher or lower notes.

TROMBONE

Slider

Slider pulled out makes a lower note

XYLOPHONE

Percussion instruments use larger or longer vibrating objects to produce lower notes.

Longer blocks produce lower notes

Shorter blocks produce higher notes

The Doppler effect
The pitch of a sound made by an object will also depend on whether the object is moving toward or away from you. This is known as the Doppler effect.

Sound waves bunched together

If an object is moving away from you, sound waves are stretched out, making the pitch lower.

If an object is moving towards you, sounds waves are compressed, pushing the pitch up.

9

THE SPEED OF SOUND

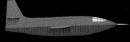

Bell X-1 – Mach 1.06

Sound takes time to travel from its source and the speed at which it moves depends on what it has to travel through. The more dense the medium, the faster it will move. This is because the particles transmitting the sound wave are more tightly packed together and will pass on the energy of the sound wave more quickly.

In dry air at 32°F (0°C), sound travels at 1,086.9 feet per second (331.29 m/s).

In water at 46.4°F (8°C), sound travels at 4,721 feet per second (1,439 m/s).

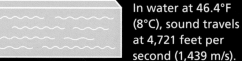

Through glass, sound travels at 14,895 feet per second (4,540 m/s).

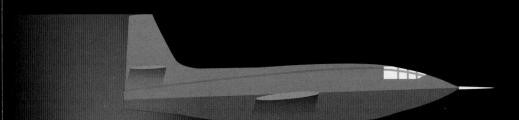

In October 1947, American pilot Chuck Yeager flying his Bell X-1 rocket-powered aircraft became the first person to travel faster than the speed of sound.

The speed of sound is measured using Mach numbers. Mach 1 represents the speed of sound, Mach 2 represents twice the speed of sound, and so on.

Mach 1

1

Subsonic
Slower than the speed of sound (less then Mach 0.8)

SUPERSONIC FLIERS

Since the speed of sound was first broken, aircraft designers have created faster and faster planes, from large passenger aircraft to cutting-edge experimental flying machines.

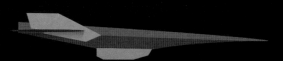

X-43A (fastest aircraft) – Mach 9.8

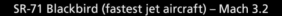

Concorde (fastest passenger aircraft) – Mach 2.04

SR-71 Blackbird (fastest jet aircraft) – Mach 3.2

X-15 (fastest manned aircraft) – Mach 6.7

Thunder and lightning

Sound will travel 1 kilometer in about 3 seconds. You can use this figure to work out how far away a thunderstorm is. Time the number of seconds between a flash of lightning and when you hear the thunder. Divide the number of seconds by three and that's how far away the storm is in kilometers.

9 seconds = 3 kilometers

Mach 2

Mach 5

Mach 10

2 5 10

Supersonic
Faster than the speed of sound (Mach 1.2–Mach 5)

Hypersonic
Much faster than the speed of sound (Mach 5–Mach 10)

USING SOUNDS

As well as telling us about what's going on in the world around us, we can use sounds to look inside objects. Some animals even use sound waves to hunt for prey when it's too dark to see.

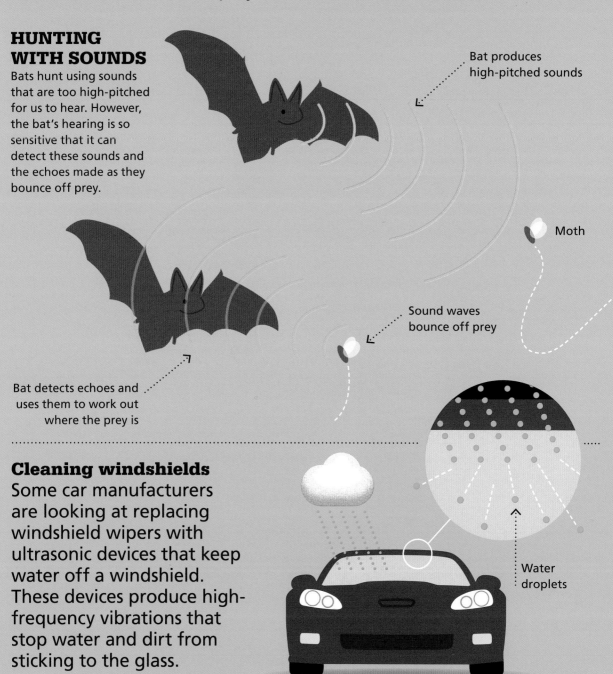

HUNTING WITH SOUNDS

Bats hunt using sounds that are too high-pitched for us to hear. However, the bat's hearing is so sensitive that it can detect these sounds and the echoes made as they bounce off prey.

Bat produces high-pitched sounds

Moth

Sound waves bounce off prey

Bat detects echoes and uses them to work out where the prey is

Cleaning windshields

Some car manufacturers are looking at replacing windshield wipers with ultrasonic devices that keep water off a windshield. These devices produce high-frequency vibrations that stop water and dirt from sticking to the glass.

Water droplets

See inside
Doctors can use sounds to "see" inside a patient to check that body parts are working properly.

Ultrasound machine produces high-frequency sounds

Probe detects reflected sound waves

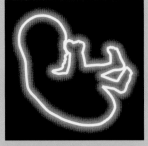

Sounds travel through body

Distance each echo travels

Reflected sound waves

The machine works out the distance each echo travels and uses this to build up a picture of what's inside.

OTHER SOUND USES
Doctors can use sound waves to shatter kidney stones and gallbladder stones so that surgery isn't needed to remove them.

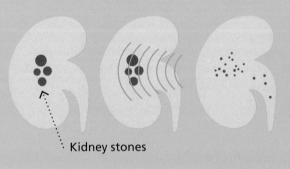

Kidney stones

WHALE SONG
Some whales make low-pitched sounds that are so loud they can carry more than 1,615 miles (2,600 km) through water. So a whale making a noise off the coast of Puerto Rico could be heard off the coast of Newfoundland.

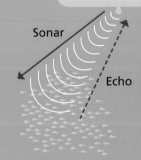

Sonar

Echo

Sonar is used by fishermen to locate fish and by the navy to spot enemy submarines. Sonar equipment makes sound waves that travel though water and bounce off objects.

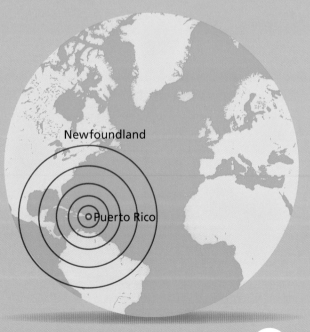

Newfoundland

Puerto Rico

MAKING LIGHT

With the flick of a switch, you can turn a dark room into a brightly lit one. The light produced by a bulb or by the sun is a form of energy that our eyes can detect and we can see.

Wave or particle?

Light is difficult to explain one way or the other. Scientists sometimes describe it behaving like a wave and sometimes it acts like a stream of particles.

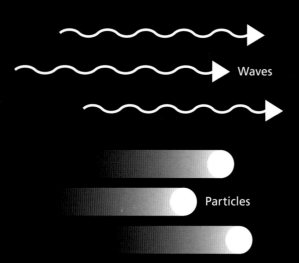

Waves

Particles

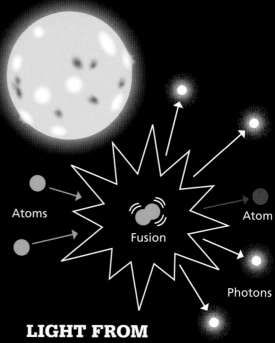

Atoms

Fusion

Atom

Photons

LIGHT FROM THE SUN

Deep inside the sun, huge temperatures and powerful gravity squeeze atoms together. This process is called nuclear fusion and it releases packets of energy called photons. This energy is the light we see.

1,000,000

The number of years some scientists think it takes light to travel from the core of the sun to its surface.

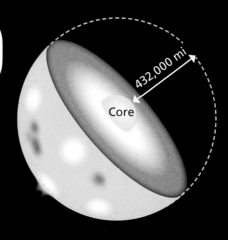

432,000 mi

Core

Absorbing and emitting

Everything is made up of tiny particles called atoms. Spinning around the center of an atom, or nucleus, are even smaller particles called electrons.

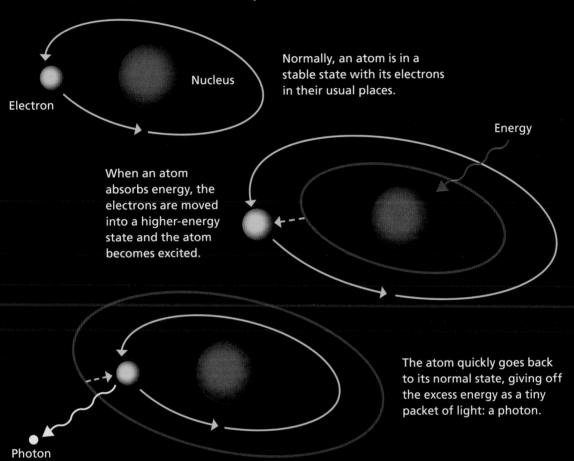

Nucleus

Electron

Normally, an atom is in a stable state with its electrons in their usual places.

Energy

When an atom absorbs energy, the electrons are moved into a higher-energy state and the atom becomes excited.

The atom quickly goes back to its normal state, giving off the excess energy as a tiny packet of light: a photon.

Photon

LIGHT BULBS

A traditional incandescent light bulb produces light by flowing electricity through a tightly wound coil. Resistance within the coil causes it to glow, but it also gives off a lot of heat.

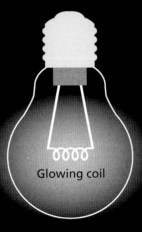

Glowing coil

Incandescent light bulb

LED light bulb

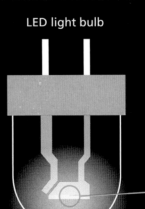

Energy-efficient LEDs produce light by the movement of electrons through a material called a semiconductor.

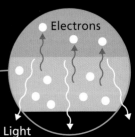
Electrons

Light

15

THE SPECTRUM OF LIGHT

Visible light forms a small part of a type of energy known as the electromagnetic spectrum. As well as the light we can see, there are other types that are invisible, such as X-rays and radio waves.

1 mm

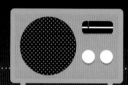

English Channel

Radio waves have the greatest wavelength, measuring from 1 mm up to 100 km, or 62 miles (as wide as the English Channel). They also have the slowest frequencies, measuring from 300 GHz (300 billion times a second) to 3 kHz (3,000 times a second).

◄ LOWER   ENERGY LEVELS ►

Radio waves
TV signals

Microwaves
Cooking, mobile phones

Infrared ·····►
Sending signals along
fiber optic cables

◄ SAFE   DANGEROUS

PROTECTING SHIELD

Some parts of the electromagnetic spectrum are harmful to us. Fortunately, Earth's atmosphere blocks parts of this harmful radiation.

Earth's atmosphere

Radio waves

Microwaves

Infrared

Visible light

Ultraviolet

X-ray

Gamma radiation

Visible light
Seeing objects

Ultraviolet (UV) light causes our skin to get darker as we get a suntan, but too much can cause skin cancer.

X-rays and gamma radiation can damage body cells, causing cell death and cancers.

HIGHER

Ultraviolet
Spotting forged bank notes

X-rays
Taking images of the inside of the human body

Gamma radiation
Killing cancer cells

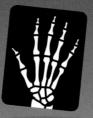

SAFE

EXTREMELY HARMFUL

COLORS

Visible light includes all of the colors, from red to violet. We can see all of these colors at once when sunlight is split by thousands of rain droplets to form a rainbow.

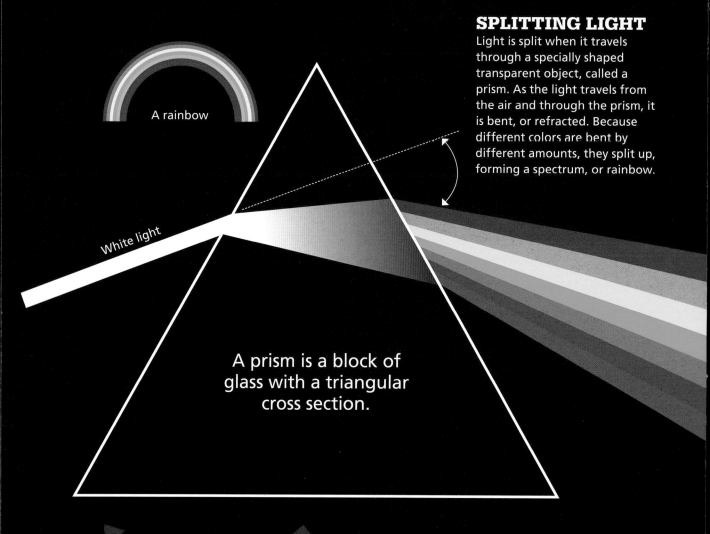

A rainbow

White light

SPLITTING LIGHT

Light is split when it travels through a specially shaped transparent object, called a prism. As the light travels from the air and through the prism, it is bent, or refracted. Because different colors are bent by different amounts, they split up, forming a spectrum, or rainbow.

A prism is a block of glass with a triangular cross section.

The red ball absorbs all the colors, but reflects red. ....>

An object has a certain color because it reflects that particular color and absorbs all the others. So a red ball absorbs all the colors of the rainbow except for red, which it reflects into our eyes.

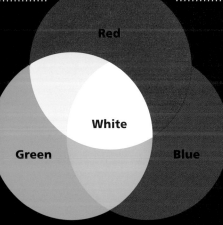

.·: Absorption line

Certain chemicals absorb wavelengths of light at specific colors. When light from these objects is split into a spectrum, there will be dark lines, called absorption lines, where these colors would be. Scientists can use these lines to see what objects are made of, even distant stars.

INKS AND LIGHTS

Mixing together lights or inks of various colors can produce all the colors of the rainbow. Televisions use a mixture of red, green and blue light to create TV pictures.

Colors with longer wavelengths, such as red, are refracted the least.

Red

White

Green

Blue

Mixing light

RED

ORANGE

YELLOW

GREEN

BLUE

INDIGO

VIOLET

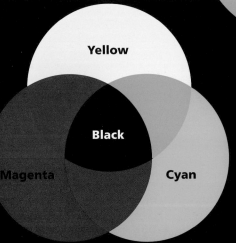

Yellow

Black

Magenta

Cyan

Mixing ink

Colors with shorter wavelengths, such as violet, are refracted the most.

.·: Dots of color

PRINTING PICTURES

Colorful books use a mixture of cyan, magenta and yellow inks. These are printed in tiny dots which are usually too small to see. These dots merge together to create thousands of different colors.

BENDING AND REFLECTING

Light travels in a straight line, but its path can be altered as it travels through different substances. Or it can be sent in an entirely different direction when it bounces off something shiny.

Lenses
We can bend rays of light using specially shaped pieces of glass, called lenses.

Refracting
When light passes from air and into glass or water, its path is bent. This is called refraction and it can make things appear bigger or smaller.

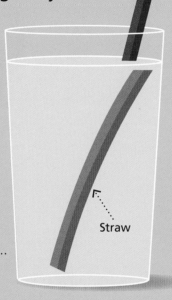

Straw

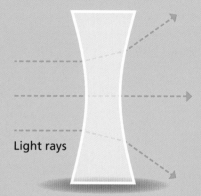

Light rays

A **concave lens** makes light rays spread out, or diverge, and they are used in binoculars and telescopes.

Clear glass

Silver atoms

Light rays

Reflected light

Black backing

HOW DOES A MIRROR WORK?
The back of a mirror is coated with a layer of silvery atoms. After light has traveled through the glass at the front of the mirror, the photons hit the silver and are absorbed by the silver atoms. The silver atoms become excited, but then become stable again, giving off energy as light, which is reflected back away from the mirror.

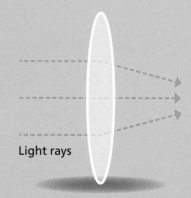

Light rays

A **convex lens** makes light rays come together, or converge, and they are used in camera lenses and magnifying glasses.

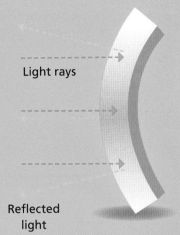

Light rays

A **convex mirror** reflects rays of light outwards and can make objects appear far away. They are found on a car's side mirrors.

Reflected light

Light rays

Reflected light

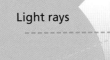

A **concave mirror** reflects rays of light inwards and can sometimes flip an image upside down. They are used to magnify objects and are found on shaving mirrors.

Bendy mirrors

As with lenses, altering the shape of a mirror will change how it reflects light.

TELESCOPES

Mirrors and lenses are used in telescopes to collect light and produce images of objects that are very far away.

Reflecting telescope

Light rays

Lens

Mirror

Mirror

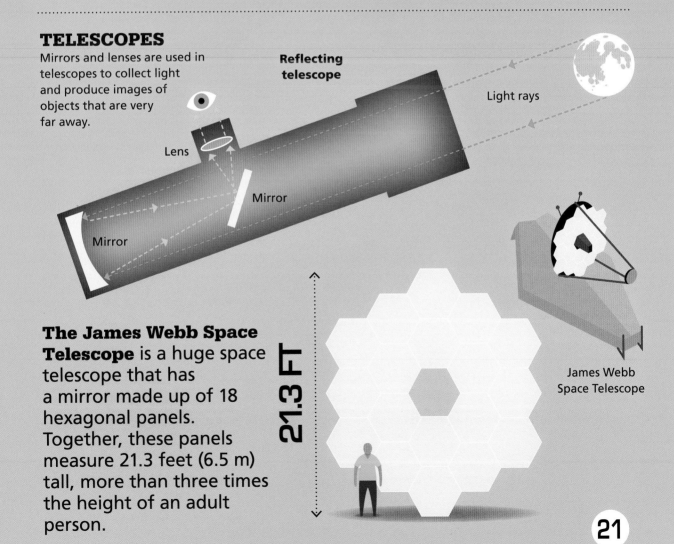

The James Webb Space Telescope is a huge space telescope that has a mirror made up of 18 hexagonal panels. Together, these panels measure 21.3 feet (6.5 m) tall, more than three times the height of an adult person.

21.3 FT

James Webb Space Telescope

SHADOWS

Because rays of light travel in straight lines, their path can be blocked by an object, creating a dark area, or shadow, behind it.

Umbra
The area of total shade at the middle of a shadow, where no light rays reach.

NEVER LOOK DIRECTLY AT THE SUN, EVEN DURING AN ECLIPSE. IT CAN PERMANENTLY DAMAGE YOUR EYES!

Penumbra
The area of half-shade around the edges of a shadow, where a few light rays reach.

Object blocking light rays

Rays of light from light source

Flashlight

Transparent objects do not make shadows, because rays of light **pass right through them.**

SPACE SHADOWS

Sometimes the moon comes between Earth and the sun, causing an eclipse. Eclipses can be partial, when only part of the sun is obscured, total, when all of the sun is hidden, or annular, when a bright ring is left around the edges of the moon.

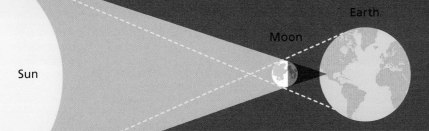

Sun

Moon

Earth

Partial eclipse

Total eclipse

Annular eclipse

The sun is 400 times larger than the moon, but it is 400 times farther away, which is why they appear to be the same size in the sky.

FINDING PLANETS

Astronomers can spot distant planets around other stars by the changes in light they cause. As the planet passes in front of its star, it will cause the star's light to dim a little, before it gets brighter again as the planet moves away.

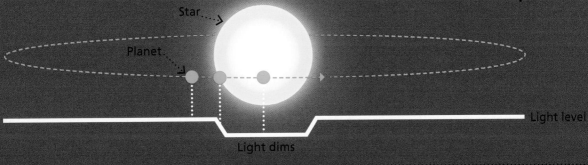

Star

Planet

Light level

Light dims

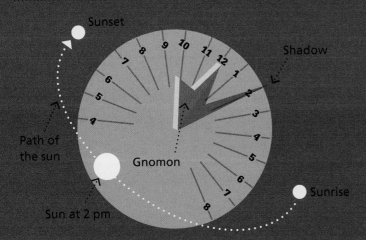

Sunset

Shadow

Path of the sun

Gnomon

Sun at 2 pm

Sunrise

Telling the time

For thousands of years, people have used shadows cast by the sun to tell the time with sundials. As the sun moves across the sky, the position of the shadow created by a pointer, or gnomon, moves.

THE SPEED OF LIGHT

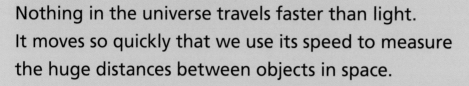

Proxima Centauri

Nothing in the universe travels faster than light. It moves so quickly that we use its speed to measure the huge distances between objects in space.

7.5 times

186,282

The number of miles that light can travel in a second. That's the same as traveling around Earth about 7.5 times.

Light may move quickly, but it still takes time to cross the enormous distances in space.

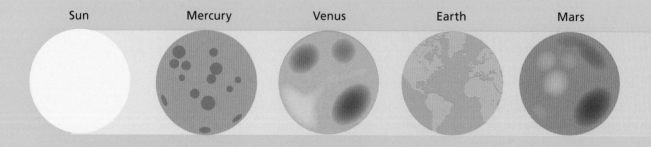

| Sun | Mercury | Venus | Earth | Mars |

3.2 minutes
Time it takes light to travel from the sun to Mercury.

6.0 minutes
Time it takes light to travel from the sun to Venus.

8.3 minutes
Time it takes light to travel from the sun to Earth.

12.6 minutes
Time it takes light to travel from the sun to Mars.

Astronomers use the distance that light travels in a year as a unit to measure the distances between stars and galaxies.

One light-year = 5.88 x 10^{12} miles

Earth

Even with this big figure, it still takes rays of light **4.22 years** to travel from Proxima Centauri, our nearest star after the sun, to Earth.

19,000
The number of years it would take a rocket using the fastest methods available to reach Proxima Centauri.

SCALE OF THE UNIVERSE

100,000 light-years
The diameter of the Milky Way.

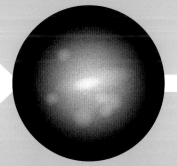

180,000 light-years
The distance to the Large Magellanic Cloud, a small companion galaxy to the Milky Way.

2.5 million light-years
The distance to the Andromeda Galaxy, the nearest major galaxy to ours.

Jupiter

Saturn

Uranus

Neptune

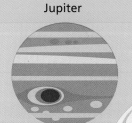

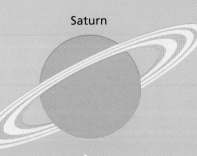

43.2 minutes
Time it takes light to travel from the sun to Jupiter.

79.3 minutes
Time it takes light to travel from the sun to Saturn.

2.6 hours
Time it takes light to travel from the sun to Uranus.

4.1 hours
Time it takes light to travel from the sun to Neptune, the outermost planet in the solar system.

USING LIGHT

As well as using light to see the world around us, we can use light to study distant objects, to send signals, to record and display images, and even to see inside human or animal bodies.

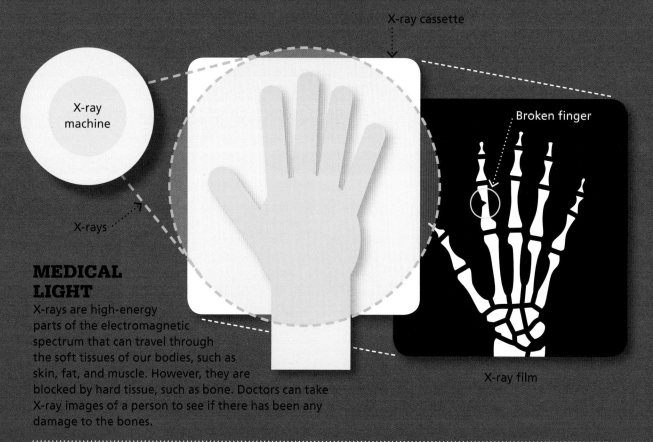

X-ray cassette

X-ray machine

X-rays

Broken finger

X-ray film

MEDICAL LIGHT

X-rays are high-energy parts of the electromagnetic spectrum that can travel through the soft tissues of our bodies, such as skin, fat, and muscle. However, they are blocked by hard tissue, such as bone. Doctors can take X-ray images of a person to see if there has been any damage to the bones.

Moving pictures

Movies and television programs create the illusion of moving images by flashing a sequence of still images or frames in front of us very quickly. Our brains string these images together to give the impression of movement.

Fiber optics

We can use light to send signals along tubes called fiber optic cables. The rays of light bounce off the walls of the cables as they travel to their destination.

Light ray

Light ray

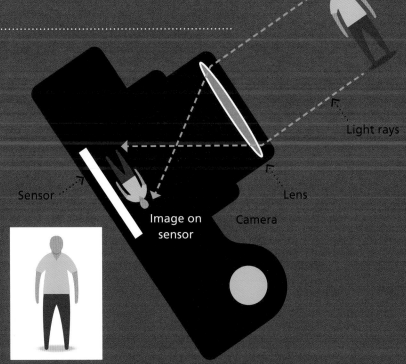

Light rays

Lens

Sensor

Image on sensor

Camera

Taking pictures

Like telescopes, cameras use lenses to collect light from objects. They focus this light onto a special sensor, which records the image as a digital photograph.

Digital photograph

18 frames per second – the rate of early movies
24 frames per second – the standard rate for movies
30 frames per second – the standard rate for many television systems
48 frames per second – the rate of slow-motion photography
300+ frames per second – high-speed cameras for very slow-motion photography
2,500+ frames per second – very high-speed cameras used for special effects

SEEING AND HEARING

While light rays and sound waves bombard us almost every minute we are awake, we need very special equipment to detect them. This equipment turns them into the sights we see and the sounds we hear.

Our eyes collect light rays and focus them to produce an image we can see.

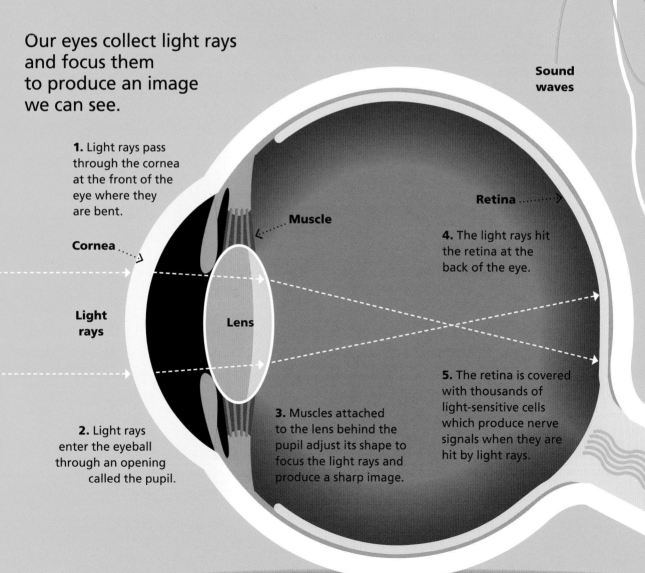

Outer ear

Sound waves

1. Light rays pass through the cornea at the front of the eye where they are bent.

Cornea

Light rays

Muscle

Lens

Retina

4. The light rays hit the retina at the back of the eye.

2. Light rays enter the eyeball through an opening called the pupil.

3. Muscles attached to the lens behind the pupil adjust its shape to focus the light rays and produce a sharp image.

5. The retina is covered with thousands of light-sensitive cells which produce nerve signals when they are hit by light rays.

Our ears collect sound waves and turn them into signals to send to our brains.

7. The nerve signals travel along the auditory nerve to the brain where they are interpreted and the sound is "heard."

Tiny bones

1. The outer ears collect sound waves and channel them into the head through the ear canal.

Auditory nerves

Cochlea

Eardrum

Oval window

2. At the end of the ear canal is the eardrum, which vibrates as the sound waves hit it.

3. The eardrum is attached to three tiny bones which transmit and magnify the vibrations.

4. The ear bones vibrate against a small oval window, which leads into the spiral-shaped cochlea.

5. When the oval window vibrates, it sends waves through a fluid inside the cochlea.

6. As the waves travel through the cochlea, they cause tiny hairs to move back and forth. The movement of these hairs triggers nerve signals.

HEARING RANGE FREQUENCIES

LOW-FREQUENCY SOUNDS

Human 31 Hz–19 kHz

Dog 64 Hz–44 kHZ

Little brown bat 10.3 Hz–115 kHz

Porpoise 75 Hz–150 kHz

Elephant 17 Hz–10.5 kHz

HIGH-FREQUENCY SOUNDS

Optic nerve

6. Nerve signals travel along the optic nerve to the brain where they are interpreted and the image is "seen."

Muscles connected to the iris (the colored part of the eye) can make the pupil larger to let in more light when it is dark, or smaller to let in less light when it is bright.

GLOSSARY

absorption lines
Black lines that appear in a spectrum showing where colors at that wavelength have been absorbed.

amplitude
The size of a sound wave, which determines how loud or soft the sound is.

atom
The smallest amount of a substance. It consists of a nucleus containing neutrons, protons, and electrons that whizz around the nucleus.

cochlea
The snail-shaped organ inside the ear, where sound vibrations are turned into nerve signals.

compressions
The parts of a sound wave where molecules are squashed together, or compressed.

cornea
The transparent layer covering the eyeball.

Doppler effect
The change in pitch made by an object moving relative to a listener. If the object is moving toward the listener, then the pitch rises. If the object is moving away from the listener, then the pitch falls.

electromagnetic spectrum
The full range of electromagnetic radiation, including visible light, X-rays, and radio waves.

electron
A small part of an atom, which whizzes around the atom's nucleus.

fiber optics
Sending messages along glass fibers using beams of light.

frequency
The number of times sound waves and light vibrate each second. The frequency of a sound determines its pitch, while the frequency of light determines its color.

iris
The colored part of the eye, which opens and closes to let more or less light into the eyeball.

lens
A curved piece of glass which bends, or refracts, light rays. It is also the part of the eye that focuses light to produce a clear image.

light-year
A unit of distance equivalent to the amount light travels in a year.

Mach
A unit of speed in comparison to the speed of sound.

nuclear fusion
Fusing two atoms together to produce a new atom. As a result of this, huge amounts of energy are given off.

nucleus
The central part of an atom, which is made up of neutrons and protons.

penumbra
An area of half shadow that usually lies around an area of full shadow, called the umbra.

photon
A packet of light energy.

pitch
How high or low a sound is.

pupil
The black hole at the center of the eye which lets light into the eyeball.

rarefactions
The parts of a sound wave where molecules are far apart.

reflection
When light rays bounce off a shiny object.

refraction
When light rays are bent as they travel from one substance to another.

retina
The part at the back of the eyeball that is covered in light-sensitive cells.

sonar
Using sound waves and their echoes to detect objects.

timbre
The quality of a sound.

umbra
An area of full shadow.

wavelength
The distance between two consecutive peaks on a sound wave.

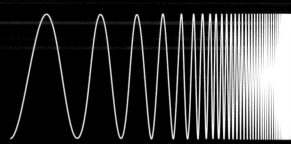

Websites

INDEX